WHAT
flyfishing
TEACHES US

P9-CJW-956

WHAT *flyfishing* TEACHES US

PHOTOGRAPHY BY DENVER BRYAN

🪟 WILLOW CREEK PRESS

© 2006 Willow Creek Press
All photographs © Denver Bryan/denverbryan.com

All Rights reserved. No part of this book may be
reproduced or transmitted in any form by any
means, electronic or mechanical, including
photocopying, recording, or by any information
storage and retrieval system, without written
permission from the Publisher.

Published by Willow Creek Press
P.O. Box 147
Minocqua, Wisconsin 54548

Design: Donnie Rubo
Printed in Canada

Soon after I embraced the sport of angling I became
convinced that I should never be able to enjoy it if
I had to rely on the cooperation of the fish.

–Sparse Grey Hackle

acceptance

By the time I turned thirty, I'd realized two important things.
One, I had to fish. Two, I had to work for a living.

–Mallory Burton

adventure

Well, this love of fly fishing takes me
places I otherwise wouldn't go.

–*Nick Lyons*

anticipation

What pleasure has fallen to our lot! Yes, there was joy in the anticipation of
the trip, in overhauling the equipment and supplying deficiencies. What zest
in planning the trip and making the engagements of guide and quarters. Long
sketches of precious enjoyment could be read from the leaves of the fly-book,
and certain flies seemed almost alive and anxious to drop into old haunts.

–*D.H. Bruce*

O, sir, doubt not that Angling is an art;
is it not an art to deceive
a Trout with an artificial Fly.

–Isaac Walton

artistry

To him, all good things—trout as
well as eternal salvation—come by
grace and grace comes by art and
art does not come easy.

–Norman MacLean

The fisherman's absorbing consciousness of water—its motions, sounds, and texture; its variety and constancy; the scope and density of life it sustains— this awareness is a habit of mind and temperament. It is a way of seeing and thinking about things, an orientation born from a mind magnetized by an irrepressible fascination with springs and creeks and rivers.

–Ted Leeson

awareness

Mark well the various seasons of the year,
How the succeeding insect race appear,
In their revolving moon one color reigns,
Which in the next the fickle trout disdains.

–John Gray

He who catches a trout has in the rough, mortal hand of him
one of nature's poems, a creature of a comeliness so rare, so strange,
so patrician, as to touch the heart of the captor with pity and with praise.

–Ben Hur Lampman

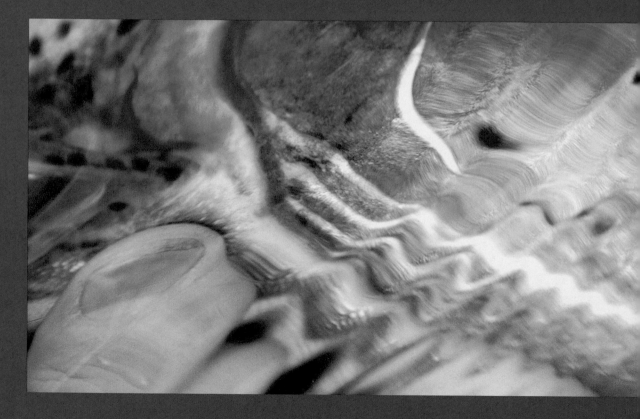

awe

The finest gift you can give to any fisherman is
to put a good fish back, and who knows if the fish
that you caught isn't someone else's gift to you?

–Lee Wulff

benevolence

Beginners may ask why one fishes if he is to release the catch.
They fail to see that the live trout, sucking in the fly and fighting the rod
is the entire point to our sport. Dead trout are just so much lifeless meat.

–Ernest G. Schwiebert, Jr.

And this our life, exempt from public haunt
Finds tongues in trees, and books in running brooks,
Sermons in stones, and good in every thing.
I would not change it.

—William Shakespeare

bliss

Up i' the early morning,
Sleepy pleasures scorning,
Rod in hand and creel on back, I'm away, away!

Not a care to vex me,
Nor a fear to perplex me,
Blithe as any bird that pipes in the merry May.

Out come reel and tackle,
Out come midge and hackle,
Length of gut, like gossamer, on the south wind streaming.

Brace of palmers fine,
As ever decked a line,
Dubbed with herl and ribbed with gold, in the sunlight gleaming.

—*Thomas Westwood*

Nay, let me tell you, there may be many that have 40 times our estates, that would give the greatest part of it to be healthful and cheerful like us; who with the expense of a little money, had ate, and drank, and laughed, and angled, and sung, and slept securely; and rose next day, and cast away care, and sung, laughed and angled again; which are blessings rich men cannot purchase with all their money.

–Isaac Walton

brotherhood

We, in conclave assembled, out of a firm and abiding conviction that fly fishing as a way of angling gives to its followers the finest form of outdoor recreation and natural understanding, do hereby join in common effort in order to maintain and further fly fishing as a sport, and, through it, to promote and conserve angling resources, inspire angling literature, advance its fellowship and broaden the understanding of all anglers in the spirit of true sport.

–Preamble to the Constitution of the Federation of Fly Fishers

The sporting qualities of a fish are dependent neither on its size nor its weight, but on the efforts of concentration, the skill and mastery it demands from the fisherman.

–Charles Ritz

challenge

The fun comes, I think, as it does with just about any other act of skill, when you are properly challenged, when you are fascinated by what's difficult. I guess I fish not because it's easy, but because it's not.

–Nick Lyons

One moment your holding a dripping, sparkling fish, the next your
looking at the water seeing an image of yourself and no one else.
For a moment, you know precisely who you are.

–*Ken Marsh*

clarity

Fish sense, applied in the field, is what the old Zen masters would call enlightenment:
simply the ability to see what's right there in front of you without having to sift
through a lot of thoughts and theories and, yes, expensive fishing tackle.

–*John Gierach*

Many go fishing all their lives without knowing that it is not fish they are after.

–Henry David Thoreau

communion

Like the finest umbilicus, casting your line into water joins you to it.
The currents speak to your bones in iced tongues. The loam perfume of
conifer rot and mud attunes your nose to the local biology. You taste its
chemistry, wash your ears in its sweet white noise, let it take you back to
a time before words and teach you things language never could.

–Jessica Maxwell

comparisons

Fly fishing is such great fun, I have often felt that it really ought to be done in bed.
Not that high frolic is the only thing the pursuit of fish and the pursuit of females
have in common; these ancient sports have more going for them than just that—as I'll
now try to tell why. First off, just as both diversions are best conducted in decent
privacy, away from distracting crowds, so too the most gratifying results are best
obtained by subtlety rather than by force, by seduction rather than rape. Again, just as
both pastimes quickly pall when the conquest is too easy, so too the lures used in the
wooing, whether jewels or jassids, must be presented with the utmost skill and grace.

–Robert Traver

confidence

Confidence in a particular fly is one of the most potent
factors tending to render it successful in use.

–*Frederic M. Halford*

Success begets confidence and confidence begets success—and that
fine upward spiral is the best restoration of streamside sanity.

–*Howard T. Walden*

Rivers and their inhabitants of the watery elements are made for wise men to contemplate and for fools to pass by without consideration.

–Isaac Walton

contemplation

Fly-fishing is solitary, contemplative, misanthropic, scientific in some hands, poetic in others, and laced with conflicting aesthetic considerations. It is not even clear if catching fish is actually the point.

–John Gierach

The contentment which fills the mind of the angler at the
close of his day's sport is one of the chiefest charms in his life.

—William Cowper Prime

contentment

Blessings upon all that hate contention,
and love quietness, and virtue, and Angling.

—Isaac Walton

If I'm not going to catch anything, then
I'd rather not catch anything on flies.

–Bob Lawless

devotion

Trout fishing with a fly consists of manipulating an infinite variety of
unknown variables. That's probably what brings us to worship at this
altar. Don't pay any attention to anyone who tells you when is the best
time to fish, friend. The best time to fish is when you're fishing.

–Stephen "Salty" Saltzman

My biggest worry is that my wife (when I'm dead)
will sell my fishing gear for what I said I paid for it.

–Koos Brandt

dread

For now, I've been savoring the mystery of my unexplored brook.
I'm letting it fester and grow in my daydreams. Eventually, of course,
I'll explore the brook and learn its realities, and it will no longer
be a mystery. But for now, the daydreams are better.

—William Tapply

dreams

Now the virtue of trout fishing is that it, of all pursuits, rewards the
dreamer with the realization of his dream. The trout are more beautiful
than he remembered them as being, and the day, the scene and the
occupation are at harmony. That is why men go trout fishing.

—Ben Hur Lapman

When the hoarse roar of the creek, where it surges against the base of the crag it has washed for ages, strikes his ear, or he hears it brawling over the big stones, his step quickens, and his pulse beats louder—he is no true angler if it does not—and he is not content until he gets a glimpse of its bright rushing waters at the foot of the hill.

-Thaddeus Norris

e a g e r n e s s

My first casts are accompanied by a sense of mild desperation, fishing's equivalent of buck fever. I'm forced to remind myself there is no hurry.

–Ken Marsh

The fish and I were both stunned and disbelieving
to find ourselves connected by a line.

–William Humphrey

elation

I doubt if I shall ever outgrow the excitement bordering on panic
which I feel the instant I know I have a strong, unmanageable fish, be it
brook trout, brown trout, cutthroat, rainbow, steelhead or salmon on my line.

–Edward Weeks

equality

There is no more graceful and healthful accomplishment for a
lady than fly-fishing, and there is no reason why a lady should
not in every respect, rival a gentleman in the gentle art.

–W.C. Prime

There are matters beyond the knowledge of non-fishermen. Forests can insulate you against the woes of the world... Quick water and dark firs and the campfire's glow at dusk and the good smell of boiling tea at daybreak are inestimable things.

–Frederic F. Van de Water

escape

And who among us is there, who would not now prefer to spend an hour in the dear old wood, or follow the banks of the old brooks, to a day in any other place?

–D.H. Bruce

focus

I continually read of men who said they would be just as happy not catching trout as catching them. To me, that even then sounded like pious nonsense, and rather more of an excuse than a statement of fact. No, I want to catch them, and every time I slip on my waders and put up a fly, it is with this in mind.

—Brian Clarke

Fishing friends are long friends because the doing of it is an intense perceptive preoccupation and one that is charged with unexpected humor.

–Edward Weeks

friendship

When your fly rod breaks and your fly box is bare, it's time to quit fishing. Go sit in your chair. Light up your pipe. Pour some Glenlivet and drink 'til you're ripe. Don't worry about your rod and flies. Just sit with your buddies and tell fishing lies.

–Jimmy D. Moore

When we see them feeding regardless of our fly or dashing
off terrified at our efforts to delude them, the resentment which
the fisherman feels is almost like the anger of a madman.

–Harold Russell

frustration

On some evenings the trout cease to rise after an artificial fly has once been floated
over them; on others they continue to rise freely, but will take nothing artificial, and
the angler exhausts himself in efforts and changes of fly, working harder and more
rapidly as he becomes conscious of the approaching ends of the day.

–Viscount Grey of Fallodon

I've gone fishing thousands of times in my life, and I have never once felt unlucky or poorly paid for those hours on the water.

–*William Tapply*

gratitude

My home river does not always give me her fish, but the blessings of her company are always worth the trip.

–*Paul Schullery*

The supply of hope seems inexhaustible, and one bestows it lavishly with each cast. If the best part of the pool is reached and past without a rise, the angler begins to husband his hope a little, but remains still content, reaching forward in thoughts to the next pool, where he presently begins with fresh eagerness and confidence.

–Lord Grey of Fallodon

hope

The charm of fishing is that it is the pursuit of what is elusive but attainable, a perpetual series of occasions for hope.

–Lord Tweedsmuir

Last Sunday I fished up a certain river most of the day and through my supernal skill and encyclopedic knowledge of angling was able to take a dozen brook trout. If I had kept them I would have had the makings of a nice can of sardines.

–Sparse Grey Hackle

humility

There he stands, draped in more equipment than a telephone lineman, trying to outwit an organism with a brain no bigger than a breadcrumb, and getting licked in the process.

–Paul O'Neil

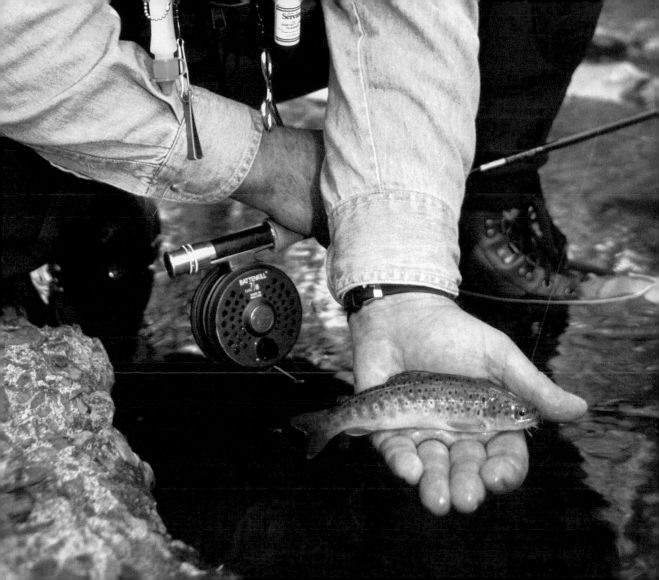

The traveler fancies he has seen the country. So he has, the outside of it at least; but the angler only sees the inside. The angler only is brought close, fact to face with the flower and bird and insect life of the rich riverbanks, the only part of the landscape where the hand of man has never interfered.

—Charles Kingsley

intimacy

Even when trout take the nymph it is difficult to time the strike so as to hook him, as most of the time the nymph is invisible and one must acquire that sixth sense which the experienced fisherman gets after years of practice of when to tighten the line.

–*Robert Traver*

intuition

Twice I had the feeling... of a sudden anticipation of catching a fish so strong that it amounts to certainty. I suppose it is partly the harmony of effective presentation when everything else is auspicious, so that a take seems in that moment to be the only feasible conclusion.

–*J.R. Hartley*

The farther you travel to fish, the worse the fishing will be. However, it will improve immediately after you leave to return home, thus the old saying: The fishing is always better the day before you got there and the day after you leave.

–Max Schulman

irony

I have never lost a little fish—yes, I'm free to say.
It was always the biggest fish I caught that got away.

–Eugene Field

Fly fishing is like sex, everyone thinks there is more than there is,
and that everyone is getting more than their share.

–Henry Kanemoto

jealousy

I fished the same places where I had done so well yesterday and caught
nothing. Another angler, fishing nearby, caught one fish after another
and played them through long runs off a screaming reel. All of them
were big fish. I looked on enviously and muttered in frustration.

–Steve Raymond

I have spent many afternoons in the shadow of ancient anglers. It is time well invested. Picking the brains of fly fishermen who are my seniors is not an uncommon practice, nor is it a bashful spectacle. In fact, the exchange of ideas and concepts within the angling community occurs most frequently through parasitic unions; the elder members are the most valued hosts.

–Don Roberts

knowledge

The best fishermen I know try not to make the same mistakes over and over again; instead they strive to make new and interesting mistakes and try to remember what they learned from them.

–John Gierach

I don't lie about the size of the fish I catch,
I just remember them bigger.

–Alan Di Soma

lying

The question is not whether successful fishermen
believe in God, but, more to the point, vice versa.

–Don Roberts

It is the glory of the art of angling that its disciples never grow old.
The muscles may relax and the beloved rod become a burden,
but the fire of enthusiasm kindled in youth is never extinguished.

—George Dawson

maturity

The time must come to all of us, who live long, when memory is more than
prospect. An angler who has reached this stage and reviews the pleasure of
life will be grateful and glad that he has been an angler, for he will look back
on days radiant with happiness, peaks of enjoyment that are no less bright
because they are lit in memory by the light of a setting sun.

—Viscount Grey of Fallodon

Now, I like to fish, but I'm a convert; I wasn't born that way.
However, unlike the addict, I can take it or leave it, and
I'd rather take it at four in the morning when a January
gale is strong enough to blow a salmon scale backwards.

—Beatrice Cook

obsession

You will search far to find a fisherman who'll admit that a taste for fishing,
like a taste for liquor, must be governed lest it come to possess its possessor.

—Sparse Grey Hackle

They say you forget your troubles on a trout stream,
but that's not quite it. What happens is that you begin to see
where your troubles fit into the grand scheme of things,
and suddenly they're just not such a big deal anymore.

—John Gierach

perspective

I held the tiny nymph on my fingertip, a mere speck I duplicated
with a clumsy fake. As I cast it into the fast-moving current, I too
became a speck, held by the expanse of beauty that surrounded me,
engulfed by a sense of peace as enormous as the nymph had been
small. Amongst the mighty scheme of things, I felt I had a place.

—Chiyo Sagara

Some go to church and think about fishing,
others go fishing and think about God.

—*Tony Blake*

piety

If fishing is a religion, fly fishing is high church.

—*Tom Brokaw*

practicality

I look into my fly box and think about all the elements I should consider in choosing the perfect fly: water temperature, what stage of development the bugs are in, what the fish are eating right now. Then I remember what a guide told me: "Ninety percent of what a trout eats is brown and fuzzy and about five-eighths of an inch long."

—Allison Moir

Angling is, or should be, essentially a philosophic and reflective engagement, rewarding the practitioner not only with trout, but with a gentler and more matured comprehension of life itself.

—*Ben Hur Lampman*

reflection

To go fishing is the chance to wash one's soul with pure air, with the rush of the brook, or with the shimmer of sun on blue water. It brings meekness and inspiration from the decency of nature, charity toward tackle-makers, patience toward fish, a mockery of profits and egos, a quieting of hate, a rejoicing that you do not have to decide a darned thing until next week. And it is discipline in the equality of men—for all men are equal before fish.

—*Herbert Hoover*

self-deprecation

April 1st, 1878—Opening day. Fished Halfway brook from Morgan brook to, and through, the woods; and then fished Ogden brook from Van Husen's road to Gleason's. Banks more than full of roily snow water; weather decidedly cold; strong wind from the northwest; cloudy sky. Caught one small trout that I returned to his native element to grow; discovered from my single specimen of the *Salvelinus fontinalis* that they have the same bright spots that they have always had; look the same, smell the same, feel the same; other peculiarities lacking. Managed to fall in the Ogden brook— in fact went in without the slightest difficulty, amid applause from the bank; discovered from my involuntary plunge that the water is just as wet as last year, and if memory serves, a trifle colder. Reached home in the evening, cold, wet, tired and hungry. Neverthless, had a most glorious time.

–A. Nelson Cheney

But, remember the back cast is the foundation, and that
unless it is solid the superstructure will be rickety.

–Henry P. Wells

technique

False casting for practice is the best way to achieve the feel of the line in the air, but
in actual fishing, false casts should be limited in number to absolute necessity. In the
first place, the more false casts you make, the greater are the chances for the fish to
see your arm waving, or the line in the air. And the greater are your chances to make
a mistake in the cast and lose your timing. Most anglers, especially tyros, false cast too
often. Three casts should be sufficient for any throw and two is better. One is perfect.

–Joe Brooks

temptation

The only way to get rid of temptation is to yield to it.

–Oscar Wilde

The greatest incitement to guilt is the hope of sinning with impunity.

–Cicero

But it is good to be zealously affected always in a good thing,
and not only when I am present with you.

–Galatians

z e a l

Zeal will do more than knowledge.

–William Hazlitt